THE COOLEST JOBS ON THE PLANET

Fashion Photographer

Justin Dallas with Rebecca Rissman

Raintree

Chicago, Illinois

Edited by Andrew Farrow, Christine Peterson, and
Helen Cox Cannons
Designed by Cynthia Akiyoshi
Original illustrations © Capstone Global Library Limited 2014
Illustrated by HL Studios
Picture research by Mica Brancic and Tracy Cummins
Production by Helen McCreath
Originated by Capstone Global Library Limited

Library of Congress Cataloging-in-Publication Data
Dallas, Justin, author.
  Fashion photographer : the coolest jobs on the planet / Justin Dallas
and Rebecca Rissman.
    pages cm. — (The coolest jobs on the planet)
  Includes bibliographical references and index.
  ISBN 978-1-4109-6641-4 (hb) — ISBN 978-1-4109-6647-6 (pb)
1. Fashion photography — Vocational guidance — Juvenile literature.
2. Dallas, Justin — Juvenile literature. 3. Photographers — Biogra-
phy — Juvenile literature. I. Rissman, Rebecca, author. II. Title.

  TR679.D35 2015
  778.9'974692'023 — dc23   2013040699

Acknowledgments
We would like to thank the following for permission to reproduce
photographs: Alamy pp. 9 bottom (© D. Hurst), 38 (© Horizons
WWP); AP PHOTO p. 39 (Matt Sayles); Getty Images pp. 10 (Image
Source/Zero Creatives), 11 (Blend Images/Hill Street Studios), 15
(Scott Gries), 18 (FilmMagic/Marc Piasecki), 20 right (Photolibrary/
Jupiterimages), 21 (Stone/Thomas Barwick), 25 (Fernanda Calfat),
40 (Elina Kechicheva/Contour Style), 41 (Fotokia); Justin Dallas
pp. 4, 5 top, 8, 16, 17, 19 top, 22 bottom (landscape), 23, 27,
28, 30, 31 top, 32, 33, 34, 35 bottom, 36, 36 & 37 (fabric), 37;
Newscom p. 29 top (EPA/BERND WUESTNECK); Shutterstock pp. 5
bottom, 20 left & 29 bottom (all Kletr), 7 (Maridav), 9
top (tulpahn), 12 & 13 (both wavebreakmedia), 14 (SeanPavone-
Photo), 22 bottom left & right (both meunierd), 22 middle, woman
(Kiselev Andrey Valerevich), 22 middle, couple (Nejron Photo),
22 middle, landscape 1 (meunierd), landscape 2 (WOLF AVNI),
landscape 3 (Luisa Puccini), woman in hat (Nejron Photo), 22 top,
braid 1 (Stock Avalanche), braid 2 (AlexSmith), braid 3 (Gladskikh
Tatiana), 22 top right (Subbotina Anna), 23 middle, landscape 4
(Andre Klopper), 24, 26 & 34 left (all DeSerg), 31 bottom (Szantai
Istvan), 34 top (Africa Studio), 35 top (Nyvlt-art), 42 bottom
(Jon Le-Bon), 42 right (akiyoko), 43 left (Jeff Lueders), 43 right
(cobalt88); Wikipedia p. 6 (Tate, London, 2011). Design elements
Shutterstock.

Cover photo of a photographer taking shots of models reproduced
with permission of Getty Images/The Image Bank/Cultura/Marcel
Weber.

Every effort has been made to contact copyright holders of material
reproduced in this book. Any omissions will be rectified in subsequent
printings if notice is given to the publisher.

All the Internet addresses (URLs) given in this book were valid at
the time of going to press. However, due to the dynamic nature
of the Internet, some addresses may have changed, or sites may
have changed or ceased to exist since publication. While the author
and publisher regret any inconvenience this may cause readers, no
responsibility for any such changes can be accepted by either the
author or the publisher.

Contents

Picture Perfect Snapshot

It was a bright and sunny day off the coast of South Africa. I had only been working as a fashion photographer for one year, and I was about to shoot a very famous model named Megan Coleman. She was represented by a large and important modeling agency that I wanted to impress. I was feeling nervous.

Megan Coleman had just won the title of Miss South Africa when I took this photo of her.

Fashion photography can be a tough job for someone who is shy, like me.

The shoot took place on a beautiful, white yacht in the middle of the day. I didn't have enough experience with photography yet to realize how the light from the white ship and bright sun would affect my photos. I could hardly see the model in my images! I nervously experimented with different camera settings and angles. Finally, I found a way to capture some great shots. Phew!

NOTE TO SELF

Fashion photographers need to feel confident meeting new people, directing teams, and standing up for their ideas. Even though it would be easier for me to work alone or in very small groups, I know that challenging myself to be more outgoing makes me a better photographer.

Growing Up

When I was young, I knew I wanted an art-focused career. My high school in South Africa had an amazing arts program that taught me more than just painting and drawing. I was able to learn about printmaking, art history, and art theory. I learned some basic photography skills, but I was more interested in digital art and printmaking. I loved learning about different ways to produce art, such as screen-printing.

Subjects like science and mathematics weren't very appealing to me in school. Luckily, my teachers recognized my commitment to learning about art. They even gave me a key to the school's art studio. This made it easy for me to drop by whenever I wanted to work on my own. It also gave me the feeling that my teachers trusted me.

This painting shows Ophelia, a character from one of William Shakespeare's plays.

TRY IT OUT!

One of the most important skills a photographer can have is learning the right time of day to shoot for the best lighting. Photographers call the hour after sunrise and the hour before sunset the "golden hours." This is because the light is the softest and most flattering at these times of day. I only wish I had known this earlier in my career—it might have saved me a few headaches!

My hero!
John Everett Millais
(1829–1896)

When I first saw John Everett Millais's painting *Ophelia*, I was incredibly inspired. I loved the colors, details, and composition. But even more, I loved that his painting made me feel as though I were walking into a story.

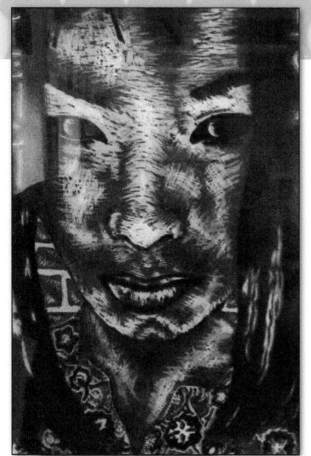

This print won the National Art Prize!

WINNING AN AWARD

When I was 15 years old, I entered some of my artwork into a very big art competition. One of my prints won a National Art Prize! This award helped me show some of my artwork in exhibitions around South Africa and in France. It was an incredible opportunity for someone so young to get international exposure. I even managed to sell a few pieces in one of the exhibitions!

My hero!
Kevin Jenkins

One of my instructors at Durban High School was a very big influence on me. Working with different printing techniques could be expensive. Students were supposed to pay for the materials they used on each project. Mr. Jenkins arranged for all of my art supplies to be paid for, so that I could create as freely as I liked.

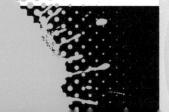

Because I was focused on digital art and printmaking, I got very little experience with photography in school. I didn't get much at home, either. My grandfather had a Polaroid camera he occasionally used. The photos that immediately printed from the bulky camera fascinated me. I loved watching them develop.

Words of wisdom

Find what interests you and spend time working on it. Tell your teachers if you have a particular passion. They might be able to give you special access to school facilities. They might also be able to teach you extra tricks to help you develop your skills.

I was never allowed to use my grandfather's Polaroid camera. The film was too expensive!

AFTER SCHOOL

By the time I finished school, I knew I wanted to become a graphic designer at an advertising agency. Advertising agencies are companies that create advertisements for other businesses. They might make billboards, television commercials, magazine ads, or any other type of promotional material. Graphic designers work on computers to create, edit, and alter graphic art. They work with text and typography. Some graphic artists also work with moving images, such as film or animation.

Learning about graphic design was a great way to get exposed to different modern artistic styles. It also showed me how important visuals are in advertisements.

Instead of choosing one of South Africa's typical three-year graphic design college programs, I enrolled in an extremely difficult and fast-paced program to earn a degree in design in only one year. Finishing in such a short amount of time meant that I had to work very hard. However, it meant that I was able to start my career a full two years before students who followed a more traditional educational program.

My fast-paced design education meant that I worked long hours and had no vacations.

Words of wisdom

The long hours of my graphic design degree helped prepare me for work in the fashion industry. Photo shoots can last from the early morning until the evening and often continue for several days in a row. Learning to work efficiently for long stretches of time in college has helped me to tackle especially tough photo shoots now.

Getting a Foot in the Door

Right after college, I started working at advertising agencies as a graphic designer. I really liked the jobs, but after a few years, I found myself working as a graphic designer and retoucher for a professional photographer. I loved going to shoots with him and learning about how he worked. I also spent a lot of time reading photographic magazines and learning about the industry.

Working in advertising gave me a hands-on education in design and photography.

After working for other people for eight years, I started my own advertising business. I often needed photographs for our advertisements. My business partner and I tried hiring photographers for projects, but it wasn't always easy. I often became frustrated when photographers didn't understand what we wanted or couldn't work as quickly as we needed. Soon, I started taking the photos myself.

Reading industry magazines and web sites can be extremely helpful. They show the current trends and new technology, and they highlight leaders in the industry. They can also be good resources for learning new ways to use your camera or software.

Did you know?

Many different people work at advertising agencies, including:

- An art director, who is in charge of all the artwork produced by the agency, including photographs and digital art
- A photographer, who takes photos to be used in advertisements
- A graphic designer, who creates and edits the art and animation for advertisements
- An account manager, who interacts with clients and finds new customers.

Fashion Photography

Most photographers start out working on several different types of photography, such as weddings or food photography. I was a bit different. I knew that I wanted to focus on fashion photography. Fashion photographers work with models, clothing designers, and beauty companies. Their work can appear in fashion magazines, billboards, web sites, or even on television.

NOTE TO SELF

Find a unique approach to photography, such as a distinct style of posing your models or always using a particular color palette. Then perfect it. This can become your signature. When agents or clients think of you, they will know exactly what they can expect from your work. This is a great way to stand out from the crowd.

Models and photographers use portfolios, which are collections of their best photos, to show potential clients the range and quality of their work.

Words of wisdom

In my first year as a photographer, I did between 85 and 100 photo shoots with local models and friends to build my portfolio. Taking photos of as many models as possible had two great outcomes: first, I improved my photography skills, and second, I met many people in the fashion photography industry.

Breaking into the world of fashion photography can be intimidating. There are few full-time jobs with major companies. Competition for these jobs is fierce. I found my way into the industry by arranging many "image for trade" photo shoots. These photo shoots are trades, or exchanges. The model isn't paid, and neither is the photographer. But both get to keep the images for their own portfolios.

My Big Break

I had only worked as a photographer for three years when I got my big break. A local cosmetics company selected three photographers to shoot its promotional materials, and I was one of them! This client was not only famous, but it also gave me creative freedom to do whatever I wanted. I was thrilled!

Up to 20 people can work on a photo shoot. This was my biggest shoot yet—14 people worked on it!

Did you know?

Whenever I get a new job, I sign a contract with the company that hires me. This clarifies my role, responsibilities, and schedule. Sometimes it even states the number of images I need to shoot.

I decided to have fun playing with different patterns in my photographs. I was given a small budget, so I purchased patterned fabric for the background. I also hired an excellent stylist (shown here). We decided to dress the models in bright, patterned clothing. We even stenciled fake tattoos on their skin. The end result was bright, bold, and beautiful. I knew that all of my experience in graphic design and advertising had helped me come up with such a complete concept.

NOTE TO SELF

Photographers must be very responsible. If they lose images from a day-long shoot, their mistake could cost them money. Many photographers use more than one method of backing up photos to make sure that they don't get lost, even if a computer or camera is stolen or broken. In addition to storing images on their computers, many photographers also rely on external hard drives and remote storage.

Work, Work, Work

work, work, work, work, work, work, work, work

Fashion photographers are very busy people. I only spend about 5 percent of my time taking actual photographs. The rest of my time is spent on other tasks. I spend a lot of time researching trends in photography by reading specialized blogs, web sites, and magazines. I think that studying the work of other people can be a great way to become inspired.

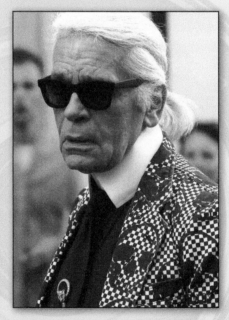

My hero!
Karl Lagerfeld (born 1933)

One of my favorite fashion designers is Karl Lagerfeld. He designs clothing for the luxury brand Chanel. He is also a photographer. If you can believe it, he has even worked as the lead fashion photographer for some of his own collections!

I also read as much as I can about the fashion industry. Trends in fashion photography change nearly as much as the fashions themselves! I look at the ads in fashion magazines as well as the editorial pages. Both of these can tell me a lot about what is popular. I look at which models are being used, how they are being posed, and what the photographer has done to capture a mood or feeling.

Did you know?

Many fashion photographers work as freelancers. This means that they work on their own. Advertising agencies and modeling agencies hire them for small jobs, such as photo shoots or ad campaigns. Unlike photographers who have full-time jobs with companies, freelance photographers work with different people and on different projects all the time.

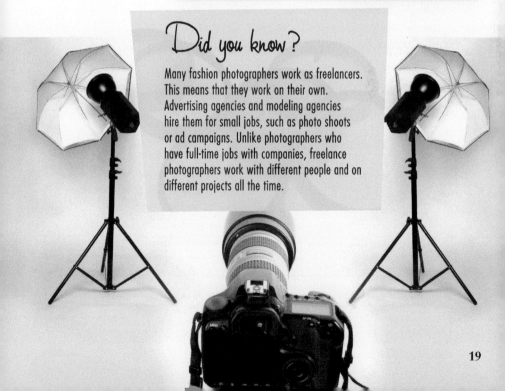

19

Meet and Greet

Networking, or building a community of colleagues, is a big part of my career.

A big part of my job is meeting with other fashion professionals. I spend quite a bit of time talking to models and their agents, or representatives. In fact, I am contacted by almost 40 hopeful models and modeling agencies each day! They are looking for someone to take their photos to help build their portfolios. As much as I would like to help them all, I just don't have the time. I am very selective about whom I work with.

Before any big photo shoot, I like to meet with production companies, clients, and modeling agencies to discuss our ideas. This is a good way to make sure that everyone involved understands the project. It also helps ensure that everyone agrees on the type of images we hope to get. After our initial meeting, I often continue to share ideas with the team using e-mail, Pinterest, and closed Facebook groups.

NOTE TO SELF

One of the hardest parts of my job is staying true to my ideas. Sometimes models or stylists have a specific idea about what they think should be done. I always try to give people a chance to share their ideas. However, I also do my best to make sure that the photographs align with my original concept.

PREPARING FOR A SHOOT

I spend a lot of time getting ready for photo shoots. I research the best locations for each shoot. For example, I might try to shoot a beauty image in an elegant old home. Once I've decided on the location, I make mood boards for each team member. Mood boards are collections of images, words, and phrases that help capture the look and feel that I want to achieve with the shoot. I often use them to show the kind of lighting, angles, and poses I'm hoping to shoot. Mood boards help make sure that the entire team understands my vision.

Hair:
Option 1: Braided & loose style middle parting?
Option 2: texture, crimped, sculptural & very architectural.

Hair is alot of texture, with tribal element implied ...
I dont want to have this too tied down to Zulu/Xhosa etc...
Just lots of detail,

Location:
Open plain veld... possibly Ballito/Umhloti in case fields ... or at PheZulu Safari Park with mountains in background.

Location needs to be practical more than anything need open fields or mountain background

Additional Notes:
Model will look as though she is doing normal rural village activities ie: carrying lamb on shoulders (ref Lebedev), or holding chicken upside down by feet ... possibly chickens running around her – maybe even Zebra in distance? She could also be leaning on a long walking pole (stick or spear) – as If tending goats?
Could be carrying a bundle of sticks – maybe even have a small fire next to her?
Maybe standing on 1 leg (like Masia do on watch) – or jumping?

Hand toning to create a Euro look (Vogue)

Post Processing
Final images to be processed in a euro style, slightly desaturated - hi impact, cimema colouring possibly.

Create a digital or paper mood board for your next project. Brainstorm your ideas about the "mood" or feeling of the project and then collect images, words, and phrases that help you capture that mood. Paste them onto a digital or paper "board."

This setting was perfect for a safari-themed shoot.

NOTE TO SELF

One task I never thought I'd spend time on is watching the weather. In the days before an outdoor photo shoot, I'm constantly checking the forecast. Rain, snow, wind, or even heat can ruin a shoot.

The day before a shoot, I pack all of my own supplies, as well as any supplies my team members might need. I bring my camera, flash, tripod, and any other photographic equipment. I also bring extra clothes for myself and food and water. You never know what might happen!

One shoot by the numbers

You might be surprised by how many photos I take to get the right shot. These numbers show how many photos are typical for a day of work.

I take 1,200 photos

1,200

I select 12 of my favorites

12

I give the client 8–10 final photos

8~10

The client uses 2–3 photos in its ads

2~3

SHOOTING STORIES

In some photo shoots, I only need to photograph one thing, such as a model's shoes. I can take photographs from different angles and in different light to find the best shot. At other times, I shoot "stories," or several images of different outfits in a collection. The outfits are all slightly different, but they might have similar colors, fabrics, or feels. It's my job to create a story that shows how each unique outfit adds up to a complete collection. Stories can be made up of two images. Or they can be 20 or more images!

Shooting stories takes a lot of organization. If I have a large story to shoot, I often have only 15 minutes between images, so I need my team to work together to switch out backgrounds, models, lighting, and props. Even the slightest mistake can cause huge delays.

These models are wearing different looks from the same collection.

MEET THE TEAM!

These are the people who often come to fashion photo shoots:

- Model: Poses for photos
- Photographer: Takes photos
- Makeup artist: Does the model's makeup
- Hair stylist: Styles the model's hair
- Wardrobe stylist: Makes sure that the clothing for the shoot looks good
- Client: Representative of the company purchasing the photo shoot. The client hires the advertising agency to create its advertisements.
- Art director: Works for advertising agency to make sure the photo shoot goes according to plan. The advertising agency hires the production company.
- Production company representative: Hires the models and pays for location fees and transportation.

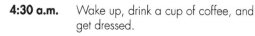

It's a good thing I love what I do, because it's hard work! Here's what an average day on a fashion shoot looks like for a fashion photographer.

4:30 a.m.	Wake up, drink a cup of coffee, and get dressed.
4:45 a.m.	Text the stylist or art director to make sure they're up, too!
5:00 a.m.	Meet my team at a convenient location. Drive together to the shoot location to make sure nobody gets lost!
5:30 a.m.	Makeup artists and hair stylists start working on models. While they do this, I start working with lighting.
6:00 a.m.–10:00 a.m.	It's show time! I take photographs of the models. We start early, to take advantage of the great morning light.
10:30 a.m.	Break for snacks. I quickly eat while I back up the photos from my camera onto my computer.
11:00 a.m.	Take close-up beauty photographs of models.
12:00 p.m.	We're finished! Pack the gear up, thank the team, and back up new photographs on my computer.
1:00 p.m.	Eat lunch. I'm usually really hungry by this time!
2:00 p.m.	Go back to my studio. Begin downloading images and backing up files.
3:00 p.m.	Select a few of my favorite images and send them to the team to congratulate them on a job well done.
4:00 p.m.	Start preparing for the next day's shoot!

NOTE TO SELF

I try not to do any editing work on the day of a photo shoot. I find that if I'm tired after a long shoot, I may lose focus in the editing. It's much better if I wait a day or two before editing or retouching the images. I make sure that all the images are downloaded and secure immediately after a shoot.

This photo shoot took place in a beautiful African setting.

These makeup artists are hard at work, even though it is very early!

Photography Tools

Some photographers like to use many different types of cameras for different settings or moods. Others work with just one or two cameras that they really like. I use a digital SLR camera. "SLR" stands for "Single Lens Reflex." SLR cameras usually have lenses that can be switched. Another type of camera some photographers use is called a digital point-and-shoot. These cameras do not have removable lenses. They are very easy to use. Some photographers use film cameras. Instead of producing digital images, these cameras capture images on film that needs to be developed.

Photographers use many additional tools to enhance their photos. Filters can be attached to cameras to change the appearance of the images. Some filters make the images look soft by slightly blurring the edges. Other filters can alter the colors and light of the image.

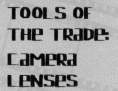

There are many different kinds of camera lenses. Some lenses are used for very close-up images. Others can be used to zoom into subjects that are very far away. Some lenses are designed for wide angles. Choosing the right lens for an image is part of a photographer's job.

My hero!
Paolo Roversi
(born 1947)

Paolo Roversi is an Italian photographer I admire. He likes to work with a very unusual camera: an extremely large and heavy Polaroid. Each 8-by-10-inch photo Roversi prints with his old camera takes several minutes to develop. His slow and careful work results in extremely beautiful and unusual shots.

My Skills

You might think that the most important skills a fashion photographer can have involve a camera, but you'd be wrong! The skills I have worked hardest to develop are my communication skills. Working as part of a team can be challenging. It is often the photographer's job to keep everything running smoothly.

I tell models how to pose and what emotions to show.

TOOLS OF THE TRADE: COMPUTER SOFTWARE

Computer software makes selecting photos from a shoot fast and easy. During a shoot, I often allow clients or art directors to use a tablet computer, camera preview screen, or a digital image viewer to mark images they strongly prefer. Then, when I'm sorting through the thousands of photos from a day-long shoot, I can quickly see their favorites.

Many people working on a photo shoot are paid by the hour. This means everyone has to work quickly and efficiently in order to stay on budget!

Disagreements about the look or feel of a shoot can quickly make things tense. I try hard to make sure that everyone working on a photo shoot gets along. The fashion industry is small. I have worked with the same individuals many different times. It is important to make sure that we have a good relationship, because it makes future jobs run more smoothly!

Did you know?

Many models also work as makeup artists! Some photo shoots and fashion shows involve 30 models or more. Adding an additional 30 makeup artists to the mix would be too complicated and chaotic. Instead, many photographers prefer to work with models who can do their own makeup.

MASTERING TECHNIQUES

Computer skills are also very important for photographers. After I take my photos, I work on the computer to edit and retouch them. I might correct the lighting or apply a filter to an image. Sometimes I use a computer to create composite images. This means that I take parts of different photos and paste them together in one final image.

This is a composite image. Compositing is a popular technique because it allows photographers to make sure every element in an image looks perfect.

TOOLS OF THE TRADE: MORE SOFTWARE

There are several software programs that help photographers manage and develop their high-resolution images, such as Apple Aperture, Adobe Lightroom, or Capture One. Photographers can use them to balance color or experiment with filters or visual effects. These programs can also be used to share files with people in other locations. I primarily use these programs as a way to show clients images and to select my favorites.

No amount of computer editing or retouching can make a bad photograph good. This means that it is still very important to understand how to take good photographs. The lighting and composition, or arrangement, of a photograph is very important. If they are off, no amount of editing or retouching will save the photograph.

I worked hard to get the lighting just right for this photo shoot.

WHAT DO YOU THINK?

Some photographers heavily retouch images before printing them. They might erase wrinkles, make models look thinner, or even change the color of a model's eyes for a stronger effect. Some people worry that this creates unrealistic expectations of beauty for both men and women.

LIGHTING MATTERS

Getting the lighting right is a very important part of a photographer's job. Luckily, we have many tools that help! One simple tool I often use is a flash. Some small flashes attach to a camera and give a burst of bright light as I take a photo. Other flashes are bigger and can be hung around a studio. These give even more light. Some photographers hang additional lights from the ceiling or from the walls. Another helpful tool is a reflector. This is a large reflective surface that bounces light in the right direction.

I used reflectors and additional lighting to get the right look for this photo shoot.

Light meters tell photographers how much light their camera can pick up from a particular subject. I use a light meter to tell me what settings to use on my camera to get the best shot.

OH NO!

One day, a photographer friend of mine was doing a photo shoot near the sea. He set his camera and tools up on his tripod and stepped away. Just then, a young boy ran past and knocked the camera, lens, and tripod into the water! A few days later, my friend recovered all of his gear. He was shocked to learn that even though the camera and lens were destroyed, his memory card had survived!

NOTE TO SELF

Camera equipment is expensive! Most photographers insure their equipment such as cameras, lenses, tripods, flashes, and lights. This means that if they lose or break something, they can get money from an insurance company to replace it.

Finding Inspiration

You can find inspiration for your art anywhere you look. The trick is to keep your inspiration organized! I keep a file of everything I find inspiring on my computer. I store photographs, paintings, videos, and songs that make me feel creative. Keeping these all in one place on my computer makes it easy for me to reference them when I need a creative boost.

I love the way some old paintings use texture to add richness. I got inspired when I saw this floral fabric below. I thought it would be the perfect way to mimic some of the beautiful old paintings I admire, so I did a floral photo shoot. Here, the stylist is setting the scene.

I also find creative inspiration in working with others. Sometimes I will work with another photographer or stylist on a fun, creative shoot for free. Or I'll invite my team of colleagues to hang around after a photo shoot has finished. Then we can have fun experimenting with new looks, poses, and photography techniques. I find that when there isn't any pressure from a client or art director, our ideas flow more freely.

I love how this image turned out—the contrasting textures make it very interesting.

TRY IT OUT!

Make your own "inspiration file." Use a folder, sketchbook, or computer file to store anything you find inspirational. Include things like photographs, web sites, songs, or videos. When you want to try something new, browse through your inspiration file and see if you get any ideas!

Admiring Photographers

Another way I find inspiration is by researching successful fashion photographers from the past. A way to do this is looking through old fashion

magazines. I can see what trends were popular and how the photographers chose to show their subjects. Sometimes it's interesting to see how photographers used light or effects to enhance their images. Other times I can find inspiration in photographers who took very simple images. I like to read biographies of these photographers to learn about their lives and what they found inspiring.

Old magazines are a great place to find inspiration. Try going to your local library and look through some fashion magazines. Pay attention to how the fashion photographs are lit, styled, and composed.

My hero!
JoeyL (born 1989)

JoeyL is a young Canadian photographer who is doing really interesting work. He photographs famous people. Recently, he photographed the actors in the *Twilight* trilogy for the movies' posters. He composited several images together to make the posters dynamic and beautiful.

I also enjoy looking at the work of modern fashion photographers. Looking through their online portfolios can be really interesting. It is a good way for me to see how modern cameras and editing technology are being used to showcase different fashions.

My hero!
Ashley Lebedev
(born 1983)

Ashley Lebedev is a fine art photographer working in Minnesota. She shoots dreamy, striking photographs of old buildings, portraits, and landscapes. Her photos make me think of the images from storybooks.

39

It's Worth It!

I love working as a fashion photographer. It is challenging, creative, and fun. I feed off the energy of models, makeup artists, stylists, and other photographers. I love meeting fashion designers and seeing their collections. I especially enjoy traveling to exotic locations for photo shoots!

Fashion photographers often get to travel to beautiful locations around the world.

I feel lucky that I am able to produce art for a career. Every time I see one of my photos in a magazine or store, I feel proud of my accomplishments.

If you enjoy fashion, looking at photography, and taking your own photos, you could be a fashion photographer. All you need is a camera, a volunteer model, and some inspiration!

Be passionate about what you shoot! The best photographs are taken by photographers who are really focused and interested in their subject.

TRY IT OUT!

My biggest piece of advice for people interested in photography is to get a camera—any camera! It doesn't matter if it's a camera on your cell phone or a nice SLR camera. Start taking photos and experimenting. Post your photos to a blog or to Facebook and invite your friends to give you constructive feedback.

READ ALL ABOUT IT!

Do some photography research of your own. Go to photography web sites and find photographers whom you admire. Then read about how those photographers work, what inspires them, and how they got their starts.

Quiz

Do you have what it takes to be a fashion photographer?

1. Do you like working with large groups of people?

a) Yes! The more, the merrier!

b) Maybe. I'm nervous around people I don't know.

c) No, I'm more of a loner.

2. Do you like researching art online?

a) Of course! That's what I do after school!

b) Sometimes. It depends on the type of art.

c) No way. I'd rather watch TV.

3. Do you find fashion interesting?

a) Yes! I read *Vogue* every month.

b) It depends. I like some types of fashions.

c) Not really. I'm more of a T-shirt and jeans kind of person.

4. Do you like taking photos?

a) Duh! Haven't you seen my Flickr page?

b) Sure. I've got a few photos on my phone.

c) I'd rather leave the photography to someone else. But I'll model any day!

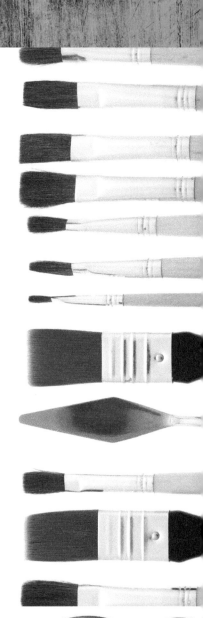

5. Do you like working on computers?

a) Totally! My laptop is right here in my bag...

b) Sometimes, especially if video games are involved.

c) No way. I prefer a paper and pen any day.

6. Are you a morning person?

a) Yes! I've been up since 5 a.m.!

b) Zzzzzz...What were you saying?

c) No way. Check in with me at noon.

If you answered mostly As...

You could be the world's next great fashion photographer! You have the passion, focus, and interest. Now you just need a little practice. If you don't own your own camera, borrow one from your school library or a friend and get shooting!

If you answered mostly Bs...

You're on the fence. You might love being a fashion photographer. Or you might be better suited for another career in the visual arts, such as graphic design or advertising.

If you answered mostly Cs...

Fashion photography might not be the best career for you. But don't worry—you can still work in fashion or visual arts if you'd like. You could be a clothing designer, a makeup artist, or a painter. Spend some time in your school's art studio and see.

Glossary

advertising agency
business that creates
advertisements for
other companies

art director person who
works for an advertising
agency to supervise all
the visual arts produced
for clients

back up copy and/or
archive material on a
computer. Backing up
prevents the loss of
data or files.

budget specific amount
of money that is set
aside for a project

collection group of
fashions created by
one designer or team
of designers to tell a
"story." Collections
can be large or
small, but all share a
theme, color scheme,
or similar fabrics.

composite image
composed of two or
more separate images.
Composite images
are often digitally
manipulated to look
as though they show
just one image.

composition
arrangement of parts
of a picture or piece
of art

editorial parts of a
magazine that are
not advertisements

exhibition public
artwork show

filter camera device
used to alter the color,
light, or sharpness
of images

flash camera
attachment that produces
a burst of light

graphic designer person
who works on computers
to create, edit, and alter
graphic art

high-resolution images
images that have a large
amount of detail visible

insure make regular
payments to an
insurance company
so that if you have
an accident or your
equipment is lost
or damaged, you
receive money or new
equipment to replace it

lens part of a camera
that gathers light for
an image

light meter device used
to determine lighting and
what camera settings will
best capture the image

modeling agency
company that represents
many fashion models

44

mood board digital file or paper board that shows a collection of inspirational elements used to organize, plan, and outline a photo shoot. Mood boards can be used to plan shoots image by image, or they can be a general resource for the look and feel of a shoot. They are sometimes called storyboards.

palette collection of colors used by an artist in a photo or painting

portfolio collection of images used to show the range, scope, and quality of an artist or model's work

promotional used to publicize something or someone

reflector large piece of material used to bounce light in the right direction for a photo shoot

representative person who represents a larger group or company

retoucher person who works to edit photographs or images to remove imperfections

SLR abbreviation used for a type of camera called a Single Lens Reflex. SLR cameras have lenses that can be swapped out.

stylist person who works with clothing, hair, makeup, and setting to design a look for a photo shoot

typography art of designing, setting, and arranging printed letters

wardrobe term used to describe the costumes or fashions worn during a photo shoot or stage production

Find Out More

BOOKS

Bidner, Jenni. *The Kids' Guide to Digital Photography.* New York: Sterling, 2011.

Miotke, Jim. *BetterPhoto Basics: The Absolute Beginner's Guide to Taking Photos Like a Pro.* New York: Amphoto, 2010.

Thomas, Isabel. *Being a Photographer* (On the Radar: Awesome Jobs). Minneapolis: Lerner, 2012.

WEB SITES

www.kodak.com/ek/US/en/Home_Main/Tips_Projects_Exchange/Learn/Top_10_Tips_for_Great_Pictures.htm
Visit Kodak's web site to learn 10 simple tips for capturing great photos.

photography.nationalgeographic.com/photography
Head to this web site for photo tips, contests, and inspiration. National Geographic is known around the world as being a great resource for photographers and photography lovers alike.

www.teenvogue.com/fashion?intcid=nav/fashion
Stay up-to-date with the latest fashion and photography trends by visiting *Teen Vogue*'s web site.

TOPIC FOR RESEARCH

Online photography tutorials and articles with tips are a great way to build your photography skills and your knowledge of photography. You'll learn new ways to use your camera, how to master different points of view, and how to get the most out of your photos. The following are great places to start:

www.digitalcameraworld.com/2012/08/16/7-beginner-photography-tutorials-that-can-still-improve-your-photography

www.pcmag.com/article2/0,2817,2399400,00.asp

www.pxleyes.com/blog/2009/06/34-essential-tutorials-to-get-started-with-digital-photography

Index